a nasty piece of work
– number one

j. andersen

◆ FriesenPress

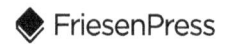

One Printers Way
Altona, MB R0G 0B0
Canada

www.friesenpress.com

Copyright © 2024 by J. Andersen (jeffscribbler@gmail.com)
First Edition — 2024

Front and back cover illustrations by Yves Cruchot (Yvescruchot@thenoise eye)

All rights reserved.

No part of this publication may be reproduced in any form, or by any means, electronic or mechanical, including photocopying, recording, or any information browsing, storage, or retrieval system, without permission in writing from FriesenPress.

ISBN
978-1-03-919827-2 (Hardcover)
978-1-03-919826-5 (Paperback)
978-1-03-919828-9 (eBook)

1. LITERARY COLLECTIONS, CANADIAN

Distributed to the trade by The Ingram Book Company

This Book is Dedicated to the Memory of

**Randall William Oberg
(August 22, 1956—February 16, 2023)**

and

**The inspiration of
Uncle Bill and Uncle Paul**

**Many thanks to
Taylor Wilson
Yves Cruchot
And
FriesenPress**

Table of Contents

Every Free Eye in the Barroom...	7
Angry Men	9
My Dinner with Andy	11
I was broke once...	17
Frank's pact with the devil...	19
Presence of Malice	23
Photocopier Training	33
A Bandit Tale	35
The Light Grey Wash of November...	39
Seeds of the Father	41
Men Cubed	47
Hamilton Poem	53
Living in an apartment...	55
Contest Time!	57

Every free eye in the barroom, all male, was turned towards the roving waitress. Cheerful and seemingly tireless, she walked the dirty carpet, asking questions and responding coquettishly to flirtatious advances. Mostly, her intrusions into the men's lives were waved, grunted, or shaken away, but for one lingering point of interest. Namely, her navel. Between the robust denim of her well-worn, but expensive blue jeans and the tied-up staff T-shirt, their stood a small field of soft, cool flesh that rose to a Rubenesque rise, capped magnificently by her belly button.

It was indeed a small, quite useless piece of human apparatus that held everyone in the tavern rapt, or at least slightly interested. The traveler need only imagine it, to succumb to wanderlust, but, as far as word had it, not one of them had ever journeyed there. Men lazily followed the navel around the room, but never a rude comment was said, at least not in the waitress's presence. Each day, when her shift finished, and she had cut enough limes and lemons, the young lady would unroll her wrinkled shirt, hiding until the next day, her abdominal triumph, and sit with her coworkers as they relaxed, smoking, drinking, engaging in shop talk. Arriving home to her one-bedroom apartment later, she would unfetter her long dark hair from its constricting elastic, take off the sensible work shoes, check her telephone messages, and remove her navel from its socket. She would give it a rinse in the bathroom sink, and then lightly deposit it into a glass of water and mild cleaning solution.

During the night, she would sleep restlessly, lightly, at first until the sound of her navel bumping rhythmically against the side of the glass like a heartbeat would lull her into the great night.

Angry Men

There are
Angry Men
On my street
Blue BMW coupe—unlicensed,
Enters and exits the neighbor's driveway.
Rapidly, again and again
In impotent fury,
Urged on by shouts in a foreign language
Grimace, rage, pout, sulk.

Across the road
An Angry Man pulls the cord of his gas powered lawnmower
As if strangling a bull elephant.
Red in the face, vein in forehead pulsing like
An umbilical cord
Savage tearing with each pull.

There are
Angry Men
On my street
And the yanking neighbor's neighbor—
Finds time between hockey games and driveway spraying
To berate his children,
Particularly his son,
Who, it seems, is incapable
Of a single correct word or deed
And is infuriating as well.

"You're doing that wrong!"
"Wrong, wrong wrong!"
"No, no! NO NO!"
"Don't do that, do this!"
"Come here right now!
Go away later!"
"Too soon! Too Late!
Not enough—too much!
Be careful! Hurry up!
"What are you waiting for?!?
You're doing everything wrong!!"
A Patricide in waiting.

I hear and see all of this,
As I set a bad example
Idling on my front porch,
Smoking a cigarette and staring at the sky…
Someone not to aspire to be…
Uncomfortably,
My stomach tightens
I can both feel
The pain of the boy
And the anger of the man.

Just because I'm not shouting,
Doesn't mean I'm not angry.
I am an angry man
Because
There are
Angry Men
On my street
And I am one.

My Dinner with Andy

The assignment was simple, the man, not so. All I had to do was spend a week poking, probing, and if necessary, pulling from him the information required. After waiting a half hour at the pub, I was about to leave, flustered, when I saw my quarry enter... sharp, exact, and malign. He headed straight towards me, glowing cigarette leading the way, hat at a jaunty angle, worn sports jacket highlighting his small frame. Extending my hand to meet his, he ignored by bodily presence completely, focusing his unseen eyes on my hip pocket.

"So, are y'gonna get the fuckin' drinks in, or wot?" he barked.

"Er... yes, yes, ...of course" I stammered, quitting my cleverly rehearsed introductory speech and matching ice-breaking jokes. I was now forced into a servile position,

"Get us a stout" said he, and I walked off to the bar, arousing the suspicions of the regular customers, who looked as if they had to be dusted from time to time. A blonde woman with thick, pouty lips eyed me suspiciously from the confines of her faux fur jacket, which was thirty years out of date, but suited her, nonetheless. Turning quickly to the long oaken bar, the roar of a darts game covered my request to the barman, who was polishing already clean pint glasses with a cloth. I had to raise my voice to meet his hairy ears. Nodding, he returned with two fresh pints.

"That'll be four and twelve," he said, taking my five-pound note, and depositing the change on the clean, dry bar.

"And just one other thing, if you don't mind?" which I didn't, eager to gain information from any and all sources,

"Why on Earth would anyone want to interview HIM?" he asked, pointing to my subject, who was now slouched in a corner bench, signaling his impatience clearly by tapping his foot. The best answer I could manage was,

"Well, er… it's just that he's sort of a… 'cult figure' in other parts of the world. And he's never granted an interview before. Until now…" I beamed at this last bit of information, and at this proud moment, the rather beat looking blonde laughed and blew smoke out of her pert, snub nose, "He must be really hard up this week", she snorted "'cos normally, a man like Andy Capp would've beaten the shit out of you by now!"

I forced a laugh, a grin, and a paltry wink, and a realistic exit back to the table, not wanting to keep Mr. Capp waiting.

After years of relative silence and obscurity, THE Andy Capp was about to reveal to me, your faithful reporter, his inner workings. Hopefully. He seemed a man of few words, and rather reactionary reactions. I wanted to chart the course his personality took and try to make sense of it all. A straightforward assignment enough, as it were, if he were willing, which he was about eight pints later. We came to the agreement that I would stay at his house for the week, and tag along with him as unobtrusively as possible—he made special note of this last condition by making a fist and holding it under my nose—all this, in return for buying him his libations.

By midweek, having exhausted the magazine's expense account and some of my own savings, I was nonetheless impressed, or at least awed by Andy's lifestyle, and decided to carry on with what would be my most important assignment to date, both personally and professionally. On Saturday, he managed to play an entire game of soccer with a cigarette hanging out of his mouth. Not only that, but Andy also scored six goals, and started, fought, and won three separate fights. By the end of the week, my liver swollen, we had met the milkman together on several occasions, been subsequently tossed out of the house by Flo. Flo, the light of Andy's life. Flo, patient, yet firm, long suffering, what with her husband, and the fact that she had had the same plastic curlers in her hair for well on thirty years. A routine developed. I slept uncomfortably on the floor while Andy napped—frequently and paid his bar tab every afternoon and evening. Covering his expenses like a generous blanket. I also bought drinks for Andy's friends, and the seemingly identical looking women he courted at the pub but had to make myself scarce while he romanced them up against walls in urine-soaked alleyways. I also met Andy's longtime friend and companion, Chalkie, and bought his drinks too.

The week came to an end, quietly, as we sat in the front room of the Capps' small townhouse, me thinking about the week spent together, he probably thinking about how many more drinks he could wring from my wallet. Who was this man, exactly, and why hadn't he spoken more than a few grunts to me all week? Why was he so reluctant to bare his soul, when his physical body required so little to sustain itself? And why did I have to pawn my watch, and hitchhike to the airport? As if in answer, Andy suddenly looked me up and down from his perch on the sofa,

"Let's go" he croaked, his voice strained, and he pointed in the opposite direction of his local public house. An hour later, in a distinctly uncharacteristic tea house, and refreshingly sober, Andy let Andy fall out before me. The drinking, the darts, the women, and finally, the cap. In my memory, he had never taken it off. It was on his head at every twist and turn of his rather exhaustive yet routine life. Never to be adjusted or altered in position by tumbling fights on each and every Saturday afternoon, never knocked askew by a chance meeting with Flo and her rolling pin. Never sent flying into the street as the result of a slap from one of the girls with the pert noses, bobbed hair, and fake fur jackets. I finally asked the question "Why?" why he never took his hat off, even at bedtime, and presumably bath time as well.

Tilting his head sideways, and then lowering it, Andy's delicate, nicotine-stained hand grasped the soft brim of his peaked cap. Taking a deep breath from his cigarette, he lifted the cap upwards, making a slight sucking sound, and placed it on the table, lost and lonely. Trembling slightly, I stared at the shadowy space where the hat had been. Andy broke the fearful silence with a strained, gravelly whisper,

"You want to know why I never take me cap off, you speccy bastard?" Knowing full well my answer, Andy raised his oddly pointed head, and looked at me…directly. Shaded for years behind a cheap twill hat, two bright, blue orbs, book ended by iridescent whites, with ebony pupils pinpointing an exact center stared at me with an honest intensity. Never had I seen eyelashes that long or sensuous, on man or woman, and a sparkle that glinted, even in the grim Northern dusk. Those eyes spoke reams of poetry and magic to me, and I wondered aloud why. Why had this man never shown his gift to the world, as success in the cartoon would be guaranteed, not just a marginal spot in low-level dailies? In answer, Andy shrugged and wiped a large tear from his left eye. Again, he addressed me with more words than he had used the entire week, putting his cigarette out on the table, along with, it seemed, his carefully constructed defenses.

"A long time ago…" he began, voice aquiver "I promised me mum I'd never abuse these eyes… that I'd never exploit them… 'cos some folks don't have 'em. She didn't. Not even pupils." He leaned closer to me "And her… just a poor orphan… Annie…"

I was broke once and had no choice but to roll pennies.

As luck would have it, I had no money for cardboard penny rollers, and the bank would not take them loose in a coffee can.

Forced to borrow money from a friend, his own pennies wrapped in brown paper rolls, incidentally, I purchased a set of plastic-type penny rollers in order to roll my own jangling free pennies.

Unfortunately, I began to get tired and frustrated while rolling the pennies into lots of fifty and spent a small portion of the borrowed money (originally in penny form) on a coffee, donut, and small packet of cigarettes, to the dismay of the corner store clerk.

Refreshed, I finished rolling my own pennies, now in plastic sheaths bought with borrowed pennies (see above).

Once done, I redeemed my original pennies, now acceptably rolled in plastic tubes, at the bank, who were more than happy to oblige.

Sadly, the sum of my pennies (once rolled, and now converted into vastly easier to handle paper currency) was exactly the amount owed to my friend ,loaned to me in the first place to buy penny rollers.

I paid my friend back in bills, not bothering to change the sum back into the original form into which it was loaned and found that I had nothing.

The next day, I lit my last cigarette, tipped the ashes into the empty coffee cup, and simply thought about a donut.

Frank's pact with the devil was as solid as the rock he was now chained to. In life, he had been a successful businessman, adored by women and revered by men. Lucky in love and finance, endowed with superior health and a superb golf game, Frank was a fellow others tried to emulate, or at least associate with. How fitting it was that he should receive an ironic position of lone authority in Hell. Yes, Hell—the Big Fire, "down there". Home now to Frank. With countless trillions of souls crammed together as uncomfortably as possible, one would inevitably ask the burning question. Namely, who was going to do the laundry?

"What did I ever do to deserve this?" thought Frank ruefully, already knowing the answer. He dipped another impossibly stained loincloth into a leaking pail of fetid water before him. After much agitation and bother, the garment came out looking worse than it had initially, as was the norm. Resignedly, Frank set the offensive garment upon a rickety drying rack made of human bone. There, with millions of others it hung loosely, never to dry fully in the damp atmosphere of Hades.

In his earthly, mortal life, Frank had known well the pleasures of the flesh, material items, and power over his fellow human beings—all thanks to a shadowy figure in a late-night eatery, and a couple drops of blood. Now, in this doomed and everlasting afterlife, his reality consisted of endless streams of dirty undergarments, provided without end by a multitude of innumerable souls. This grind and toil—the smell of the special soap, made from brine and intestinal by-products, the leaky washtub, dually emptying and filling with putrid, water that was more silt than anything else—seemed unending, because in fact, it was. But was time to Frank now? An abstract concept, especially to the twisted demons that delighted in poking Frank's buttocks with their pitchforks when he slowed his scrubbing for even the slightest moment.

Indeed, Frank *did* have an eternity to finish the laundry, but he was constantly rushing to complete his job. More torment came from the legions of damned souls, lined up behind him, who constantly bellowed and howled for their clothes, which all looked remarkably the same anyway, a simple, yet uncomfortable loincloth, either too big or small, depending on the size of the wearer. Clutching moldy and tattered laundry tickets in various languages and hands, the denizens of Hell waved and brandished them about, as if they were passports to another, kinder kingdom. Even if Frank did manage to connect a tattered rag to its owner, the complaints still rolled in "why, it's even dirtier then when I brought it in…", or "this isn't mine. Mine had a blood stain right… here…", a taloned fingernail pointing to the underwear in question. Exasperated, Frank would shout over the blast furnaces and inverse ceiling fans "What do you want from me…!" "I'll have it done next Tuesday… or maybe next year if you don't improve your attitude…!" But nobody was in the mood to be accommodating.

Amidst the Promethean pile of soiled and sopping rags and scrubbing madly with a brush that featured only one bristle, Frank would from time to time (and eternity also) ruminate over some of the choices he had made in his life. He should never have talked to the flower girl with the cloven hoof, and certainly never had entered into a discussion with her as she asked him in a gruff voice what he thought his soul was worth. He had naively thought that she had on a new kind of shoes, and that the question she had posed was merely some sort of pick-up line he had not heard yet. All of his friends shied away when he had shown them the contract, and know Frank knew why.

He dropped his hands for a moment and sighed "I hear in heaven every lottery ticket is a winner, and every credit card is due whenever you feel like it.". Frank was awakened suddenly from his daydreaming by having a railroad spike driven through his head. Frank shrugged off his assailant/manager and got back to work. Cursing under his breath, he looked around and realized he was not alone in his suffering—to his left, a group of lawyers with hornets' nests strapped to their heads did their best to eat an ever-increasing mound of tripe and offal, the pile fed continually by former parking enforcement officers. Sobered by this and realizing that there were worse things he could stick his hand into, Frank got back to work, busily scrubbing out an unknown stain, from an unknown eon, now taking a workmanlike pride in his endeavours.

Presence of Malice

After his supper, the boy climbed his tree and looked from his perch in the tree, the boy could see his entire neighbourhood, spread out like a model railroad, albeit a decrepit and unused one. The rails and shunting yard still exist but no train has crossed them in years. He lives with his family in one of the converted railroad buildings that are set on expanses of brown, dirty ground. Being that there are very few children of his age in the neighbourhood, he spends a lot of time alone. Mostly in one of the remaining tall trees that poke through the contaminated soil and continue to live. His face is wide, and his eyes are deep set, old and young at the same time. No one seems to notice him.

Most of the families in the neighbourhood, including his own, owe their subsistence to a couple of factories nearby. The plants run all day and all night, and the workers run to and from them at the appropriate hours. The boy could see them and make out some of the words they said as they slouch back and forth, to and from work. His own father and mother work there too, in alternating shifts. Although only eight years old, he has come to rely on himself for company. His baby brother is just that, and no fun at all.

In the past couple of weeks, during this year's summer vacation, the boy has seen several new families move into the area. Like many of the other families, they are new here, and do not speak English very well, if at all. One of the families, a dark haired, work tanned trio of father, mother, and son, are one of these new arrivals. Challenging his own shyness, the boy has tried to make a connection with the newcomer, roughly his own age, but has only been met with downcast glances of embarrassment and shoe turns in the dusty, diesel-soaked ground. The boy wasn't offended at all, realizing the language barrier, but he still wished to have a play mate. The other boy looked bored and lonely as well, wandering about his grassless yard, staring at the sky and his feet.

The boy often saw him doing this routine, although he didn't see the new kid at school during the last few weeks of the term. Finally, he gave up, and returned to his tree and his watching.

Some time later, after a glass of lemonade and an "out!" from his mother, the boy climbed the tree just in time to see an older black car drive up to his new neighbour's house. The new boy's father swung his feet from the car, planted them on the gravel, and exited, straightening himself. In the man's hand he held a length of thin rope. The father was struggling with something at the end of the rope, and finally heaved the object from the back seat. A dog. Sort of a German Shephard, a mutt, but a bouncy puppy, nonetheless. The dog bounced around the man's feet and yipped excitedly. Moments later, the boy rushed from the house, the shadow of his mother behind him, and greeted the dog in a similar playful fashion. The pair rolled to the ground in a mass of limbs and drool. Despite a small portion of jealousy, the boy's lips stretched to a toothless smile, happy that at least someone in the neighbourhood had companionship.

Over the coming weeks, the boy spent his mornings, afternoons and after suppers in the tree watching. The dog became neighbourhood property and seemed to recognize and acknowledge its community. Passerby would receive joyous yelps at the fragile fences as they moved about, and in return, the dog received bits of fat and sinew from a lunch or dinner. Almost universally, the dog was loved and spoiled.

The boy, from his tree, understood full well the almost universal sentiment. However, like any childhood, a neighbourhood wasn't complete without the archetypal "mean old man". This legend wasn't that old, but was certainly ill tempered at least, and disliked noise most of all. The boy also found it surprising that he had a wife and two small, dirty children. Unlike the boy's father, this man worked the night shift, leaving at 10pm and retuning around 8 am. When the greyish lights had come on, the boy would see him as he was climbing down the tree. Sometimes he would catch the man returning home early in the morning. The boy knew that the man was far from friendly—even his own parents didn't like him. Although the man's house was set far back from the dirt track between the houses, he would become agitated when the neighbours banged out a dent on a car, fixed a motor, or heard children playing. The boy has firsthand experience of this. One day, the boy was throwing rocks at an abandoned car, and this ignited the man's fury. Quivering, the man had appeared from nowhere, grabbed the boy's ear and dragged him, tears and all, up to his house. On the front porch, he had lectured the boy's mother and would not leave until a promise was made to keep quiet. Watching the hairy back in a muscle shirt recede down the path, the boy's mother had comforted him, telling him not to worry.

The neighbour's dog was reason enough for the boy to worry. The mean old man seemed to be in a continual shouting match with the other boy's father and mother. Fist shaking, spittle flying, and the occasional rock thrown menacingly at the dog, the neighbour channeled his anger at the animal, who took it as mere playfulness and only barked more loudly.

This self-perpetuating cycle hummed along as the summer progressed. Heat and humidity made monsters out of almost everyone and everything. Even the dog sought the shade of its owner's porch during the middle of the day. The boy enjoyed the shade of the tree and the slight, dirty breeze that blew through it. He kept a camping canteen at his side, sipping from it occasionally as he watched the haze and shimmer of August. The man was becoming more agitated now. The boy could imagine the lines of anger and frustration emanating from him, as they did from comic book villains. He sensed oncoming trouble, like he did when a student was testing the teacher's patience at school. That, or an oncoming thunderstorm.

On a windy, overcast day that still managed to be hot, the boy had to hold on with a tighter grip to the trunk of his tree. He could feel a coming storm and knew the rain would force him inside. In comparison to the tree, inside was dull and airless. Sometimes, during a storm, he would sit on the porch and watch the puddles form in the yard, only to disappear in vapour.

From his vantage point, the boy witnessed the power of natural forces. A stray leaf whipped his face, and a few drops of rain fell. The neighbour's dog, grown to twice its original size now, raced through its confines in circles, looking towards the house. The dog's boy was nowhere to be seen. The dog yelped and howled at its situation. From the rear of the yard, the sound of an angry door opening and slamming shut brought the pet to the back fence and face to face with the mean old man.

The boy could make out the mark of hardened anger on the man's face. He was not fooled by the man's feigned friendliness towards the dog. The dog, in youth and inexperience, simply placed its forepaws on the top of the rickety fence and looked questioningly at the man. Its tongue hung and tail wagged but didn't understand what the object in the man's right hand was. The boy knew. He knew what it was for, and what it would be used for. Even from a distance, he saw the determination on the face of the man. One shot. A .22 calibre bullet tore through the dog's floppy left ear. A second shot went directly into the dog's salt and pepper chest. It dropped to the ground, hurt, and confused. Two more shots solved the pain and confusion.

A tremendous thunderclap startled the boy in the tree, and he almost lost his grip. He gave a slight shout and worried that the mean man might hear him, but he was already heading back to his house, the rain on his head and back making him shine as he tucked the pistol back into his waistband. A moment later, the door closed, and the boy's mother called to him to come inside. She worried a great deal about lightning.

Two hours later, the summer storm was forgotten, and any rain had evaporated in the humidity. The boy was again at his post, watching a haze of oily vapor cross the beige backyards. Every so often, his gaze would accidentally fall on the body of the dog. The animal looked as if it were sleeping awkwardly, and would, at any moment, spring to life again to romp and play. He felt guilty about not having done more, but justified this by reminding himself he was just a kid, and therefore greatly restrained in speech and action.

As the sun turned towards the West, the boy knew it would be soon time for his father to come home and supper to be served. Just then, the back door of the neighbour's house flew open and the dark boy who lived there ran out, across the yard. Shortly after, his mother followed him, albeit more slowly. There was a hesitancy to her stride, and the boy in the tree knew why. When the pair reached the dog, they put the palms of their hands on its flank. When the mother's hand left the animal's coat, it was bloody.

With a shout she grabbed her son's elbow and tugged him back to the house. A great deal of screaming and crying arose, and within a minute, the father emerged, scratching his armpit. He too walked slowly to the dog, patted its now cooling side and came away as bloody as the mother. At a faster pace he ran to his back door, from which cries of despair and anguish could be heard.

This was enough to propel the boy in the tree to action. After all, he would just be telling the family what had happened to their dog and leaving it at that. He felt the pain of the family, especially the boy's. Even though he had never had pets of his own, he could imagine the torment. His parents had told him that all pets die, and that he would be upset, so it was best to avoid them altogether.

Climbing halfway down the tree, the boy dropped easily to the ground. He decided it would be more proper to go to the neighbour's front door rather than jump their backyard fence. Walking around his house and turning right, he slowed almost to a shuffle. Pools of rainwater had collected in the ruts and holes of the half-finished sidewalk, and he made sure to step in all of them. More of a delay tactic than an actual diversion. Walking up the pounded path to his neighbour's door, he could hear nothing. When he pulled back the screen door to knock on the wooden one, a sound of surprise came from inside, followed by soft footsteps. The mother appeared in the doorway but kept back about a foot and looked at the boy.

Using (or so he thought) the simplest words possible and a good deal of body language, the boy explained the best he could, about what had happened to the family dog. Halfway through his tale, he could see the dark eyed face of the son appear behind his mother's hip.

When the boy was finished his tale, the mother put three fingers to the side of her face, and her thumb under her chin. Her eyes softened.

"Grazie",

Was all she said before gently shutting the door.

After supper in his family's darkened kitchen, the boy went again to the backyard. Nothing had changed and he had expected this. The only difference was the plastic garbage bag in his neighbour's yard. For an instant the boy wondered what could be inside, but then answered his own question.

It was at that moment when two long, black, shiny cars came up the laneway into the boy's block. Almost no one had a car in his neighbourhood, let alone two clean ones. Turning his body to lean against the tree, the boy saw them drive up to either side of the laneway in front of the dead dog's house. With sharp clicks, doors opened and shined shoes and black socks appeared, followed by pant legs and well-dressed men. As a group, the walked to the front of the boy's neighbour's door, knocked, and waited. They all wore the same kind of hat his father wore to church on Sundays, except in better shape. While they turned their heads to scan the area, one of them engaged in conversation with the husband. The boy in the tree could not quite make out what they were saying, but he knew that it wasn't in English. But just as he had done some hours before, the boy could easily understand the replay of the charade he had played out a few hours before, now done by the father.

When he was finished, the man he was talking to tipped his hat, extended his hand and pumped the other man's offered palm twice. Sharply, the hatted man turned on his heel and walked back towards the cars, speaking loudly to the other men, and gesticulating with his index finger. In a moment, he had left in one car full of men, while the others remained in front of the neighbour's home.

The lack of visual obstacles made it easy for the boy in the tree to see the black car turn the corner and park roughly in front of the mean man's house. The men in the car exited and walked single file to the door, the finger pointing one in the lead. The boy in the tree could see them enter the house as they knocked. Perhaps they were friends? Relatives?

The answer came to the boy about a minute later. A piercing howl preceded the mother's swift exit, pulling her son like a dog on a leash behind her. From his vantage point, the boy could see that the woman had no direction in mind but away, far away. The shouts from inside the house started hoarse and aggressive, and later turned to cries of fear and then pain, and then silence.

Although young, the boy in the tree knew what had happened. He felt paralyzed by both fear and guilt. The men quickly exited the house, ignoring the stares of curious neighbours. The leader of the men straightened his hat and pulled on his blazer. The boy could see his hands were the same colour of the family's when they had found their murdered pet. They made their way back to the car with longer strides than when they had left it and cast warning glances about them as they entered the vehicle and sped off down the road. In a moment, the other car left too. Soon after, the neighbours returned to their houses, and whatever the evening might bring to them.

The woman and the boy never returned to the house. At least not that the boy knew about. An hour or so later, a police car and ambulance arrived at the house in silence. Only flashing lights and the smell of exhaust announced their arrival. The boy saw the reflection of the lights on the hall mirror and looked outside. By this time, the police were back in their car and the ambulance attendants were securing the back door of their vehicle. Without even having turned off their cars, they backed out of the rough driveway and left the home in darkness and silence.

The boy didn't go up again the tree that summer. In two short weeks it was another year of school. Sometimes, looking up from the dirty backyard, he would consider returning to his perch, but would change his mind after a couple of steps toward the tree. He had already seen enough malice in one day to last him the rest of his life. A storm, a dead dog, and the sound of violence. Life really was a mixture of fear and wonder, but mostly fear.

FOR RANDY

Photocopier Training

Buzzword Poetry—to relieve boredom at staff meetings, I would write down every single new "trending" term or phrase, and then rearrange them later, without additions. Some worked well, some didn't*

Dr Leung briefs the staff;
Canon staff will educate.
We, early identify Arsenal of tools.
Funneled data/road map/field testing/fine-tuned.
The power of caring links to total care.
Satisfy the development of needs,
Track progress quantitatively.
Customized support program.
The architecture of method, chronological record.
The measurement schedule, composite measurement,
Bundled aspects.
(Gold Stars and Red Flags)
Measurement structures, component indicators,
establishing the norms.
Maladjustment to a multicultural environment

Social support network, ethnic circles,
Support network.
Emotional literacy for boys,
Boys on the edge.

A Bandit Tale

based on actual events.

It was the first warm day of spring, and a co-worker invited me and a mutual friend for dinner and drinks. Also, to meet her new beau. We jump at the chance. The promise of a pleasant meal in the sun and the chance to meet our friend's new companion, whom she assures us we will "really like" We are protective of our friend, and generally look out for her, both at work and out. Her choice in men ranges from the mediocre to the menacing. Without her consent or knowledge, we take it upon ourselves to be her protectors, although both of us would wilt in a fight. At least we can look intimidating…

By chance my friend and I met a dozen meters from the bar/restaurant, close enough to hear the auto-curated music and clatter of dishes. Nod and smile. We stop in the street to light cigarettes and stand talking.

"Y'ever meet this guy?" my friend asks.

"Nope"

"Hope he's better than whatshisname."

"Yeah, me too"

With nothing else to say and empty stomachs, we stroll on. Past couples hand in hand, speeding sports cars just out of winter garages and lone, lonely men who've been told to go home.

Turning the corner, we reach our destination and companions. My friend vaults the half fence in a single, jaunty bound. I walk around and go in through the gate. Our female coworker hails us, and we quicken our steps to meet her. The man beside her stands and offers a hand to shake. Instinctively, I reached for it. Unfortunately, he is left-handed. A harmless mistake. Very unfortunately, he is not only left-handed, but one armed as well.

He's only got one arm!

Greetings are exchanged and we all sit.

One arm!

Don't stare!

For god's sake, stop it!!

My internal dialogue interrupts my reading of the menu. I settle for a hamburger, mostly because that's all I can think of. Besides…

How did it happen?

At birth

An accident?

It is indeed difficult to talk when consumed by curiosity. I wonder (to myself) if I'm being too obvious about the missing appendage. I try to look somewhere, anywhere, where the arm isn't, wasn't.

Drinks arrived, food served and enjoyment all around. Her new friend turned out to be a very nice fellow, and everyone had lots to talk about. No need to stare this suitor down. Well, how could you? He only had one arm.

I wonder if there's anything there?

Just a flap of skin?

A smooth rounded shoulder?

Useless little dwarf fingers?

Arg!

By this time, the sun was begging to set itself down, and forced our eyes to our feet. Fine by me. I felt like a real jerk. Here was this nice guy who I had so much in common with—music, books, etc. It was a pleasure talking to him. Naturally, I was far too polite to ask him about his missing arm.

He probably must put up with people staring all the time!

And asking stupid questions!

How does he tie his shoes...?

It didn't look like the evening was ending any time soon. Other coworkers dropped in, and things had the look of a merry meeting that would last until the last call. I felt torn by my morbid curiosity and my obsession to be a "good guy"—at least one who didn't cast aspersions about the disabled.

When they're having sex, does he...? can he...?

I guess his one arm is very strong...

No!

To set my escape, I looked at my watch a few times. The friend I had arrived with noticed this and asked me if I had to be somewhere.

"Yeah, I gotta appointment tomorrow... don't want to be a shit bag". The others at the table laughed, including the man whose name I had forgotten in favor of his notable difference. I don't think I'd ever said my goodbyes so quickly, and when I shook the lone hand of that man, I tried to avoid eye contact. He smiled, a good and healthy one, that only made me feel like more of a chump.

He knows. He knows...

He knows I've been looking at his arm.

He could beat me up, he's quite large.

Doesn't matter. who would fight with a one-armed man anyway?

"Wait up!" shouted my friend, jumping the rail again, with slightly less dexterity (one foot in a flowerpot), "I'll come with you!". Behind us, rushes of laughter.

My plan was to head to a pub a few blocks away and relax from an almost pleasant evening, I would have to lose him, or face up to being a real prick.

We walked quickly down the street, the lights on now. Strangely, we both said nothing, until we got to the pub I had intended to cowardly retreat to.

"Uh… you wanna go in for a beer?"

I was surprised. I thought he had to "go home" as well. Of course, in my desire to leave I hadn't bothered asking.

He lifted his baseball cap and ran his hand through his hair.

"Man!" he started.

So, he knew too…

Maybe he was going to tell me what an asshole I was…

"I'm glad you had to leave! I was going crazy trying not to look at that guy!"

I leaned forward in a mock questioning posture.

"I couldn't keep my fuckin' eyes off him! I kept thinking about what his arm looked like, l felt like such an asshole, and I couldn't wait to get out of there!"

"Yeah" was all that came out of me.

"He's a cool guy too! I feel like such a dick."

"Me too" I replied, and opened the pub door for him…

The light grey wash of November pushes itself impudently against the pointless sky. A thin rustle of red leaves chases a Northern wind for a few metres and falls miserably short. The cold has begun to seep in. The dampness transcends mere discomfort and soaks souls. Let Winter come. The silence comforts those who can't enjoy themselves at any time of the year. A perfect excuse not to go outside, or, to wander, wet-footed, through the hard streets, cigarette in hand, fire in brain, ash in heart. To sit for a while in a coffee shop and plan unreasonable plans. To look purposeful. People are watching. Inertia doesn't move me. Cheer up.

Seeds of the Father

I had it pretty good growing up. Mum stayed at home, and Dad was a scientist. The usual stuff, trips to Florida, house in the suburbs, no beatings—but who am I kidding? Every kid has some "issues" to deal with; otherwise, it wouldn't be a normal childhood. Beyond the usual schoolyard fears and teenage angst, I had for a father a man who compounded the embarrassment a child feels about his parents from a certain age. My father was not what you might call "ordinarily" embarrassing; he was a downright source of shame. Even going shopping with my mother was nothing in comparison. All the racks of off-sales and defective merchandise she pored through, the purchase of last years loon-pants with no zippers and rugby shirts with one arm longer than the other, were no match for Dad's antics. It seemed then, and perhaps even now, that he was deliberately trying to humiliate me at every turn. Besides being a noted agricultural scientist (which I could more than handle) he took on at his own time and expense, a side-project, walnuts. Not genetically engineering them for a better yield or anything like that, just that they were, in my father's eyes, a life-saving nut, endowed with almost supernatural healing and preventative, medicinal properties that had only begun to be discovered. To this end, he made the conscious decision to become a spokesperson for walnuts. To facilitate this, he would regularly ride his bicycle back and forth to work wearing a beige coloured jumpsuit, emblazoned with the legend "Wally Walnut" that my mother had made for him, without flinching, at his request. To make matters worse, he would strap an enormous papier-mâché walnut to his back that occasionally had to be resculpted due to the elements, and my dismay. He would talk to every and anyone about the nutritional benefits of the walnut, which might have been natural as we lived in a walnut producing area, but even walnut farmers found him oddly amusing, if not somewhat pathetic. In fact, most people laughed at him, and, in turn, me, his only son.

Oh, how I would cringe—I could see him coming from miles away, as my eyes had become attuned to his ridiculous presence from an early age. Those ridiculous tights and that stupid walnut strapped to his back. He toured schools, at no cost of course, who would pay him? And both my elementary and secondary schools were on his list. I learned early that feigning sickness was of no use, and I had to sit in assemblies, among the snickering and howls of laughter. Everyone knew that I was the "Son of Wally Walnut", which led to a series of tired but painful jokes which I won't begin to mention here, but you can imagine all you like. Other kids' dads may have been embarrassing, but mine was the worst, and I don't feel too much better about it now. I used to wish that he would just stay home and drink or something, at least that was normal. Or maybe that he could have been a football freak and couldn't understand why I wasn't interested in sports—at least I could pretend. But walnuts? No way. There was no escaping that. What I really wished people would see was the important work he had done in the field of agricultural science, increasing crop yields for starving third world countries. But all they saw was some fool in a stupid Halloween costume riding a bike with a fake walnut on his back, as if it were the world. And it was, to him, at least. At first, I just shrank back, paralyzed with humiliation, but as I grew older, I got defensive, and angry, even at my dad—especially at my dad. He wasn't a source of fun or inspiration, for me, or anybody else really—just a carnival freak on an old bicycle. He even kept a "spare" costume in the trunk of his car just in case of "emergencies" What emergencies I could never imagine. Sometimes it got so bad I wished I could just sink into the ground and never come out. When things got really bad, I wished the same for him. Of course, I felt terrible about hoping a disability on him, but I knew it would start all over again, and he would probably roll on as "Wally Walnut" on his wheelchair. I used to fantasize about his being transferred to another research facility in another town. I imagined the dinner table announcement, and how my parents would have worried about how I would cope. The few friends I had were important, but not that important. Every remark about walnuts, my father's behaviour in public, or that I, somehow, was just as keen, drove me farther and father away from him, as far as I could go, eventually. University in another province, a job in another city, and now, a family, miles away from my home.

One incident stands out in particular. It was one of those still tepid nights in fall left over from the summer. You know the ones they write songs about. I was sitting with a girl on a rock looking over the bland lake, and she had just whispered that she was beginning to get cold. I took the hint and put my arm around her. And, just like the songs, my head started to spin. Until I heard a bell, very close by. Through my teenage haze, I just tuned it out, and concentrated on the nearing face of the girl. Suddenly, she screamed, and fell of the rock. Behind her stood my father, feet planted on either side of his bike, hands on the giant walnut, looking guilty, but not apologetic. He helped me get the girl up, and naturally, she beat a hasty retreat after having the wits scared out of her by some idiot with a superhero costume on, and a walnut strapped to his back. I didn't really make any effort to pursue the girl or talk to my dad for that matter. He apologized and waffled, while I walked away, with my hands in my pockets, slouching. I can still taste the disdain in my mouth. The girl never spoke to me again, but at least had the decency not to say anything to anyone at school about the incident. She was probably just as embarrassed as I was, and I thank her for that. I don't think it was cute. I don't think of it is a humorous anecdote. I don't even want to think about it.

And it was I, inevitably, who would find him. Mum was out, and I had stayed over at a friend's house the night before. Hung over as two days, I nearly crashed through the front door, scratching the paint around the lock with my key. I almost walked right by him, between grabbing a glass of water in the kitchen, and a much-needed trip to the bathroom. I did catch sight of him, a flopping white flicker, but thankfully not in his outfit, as I went down the hall. He didn't really make a sound until I was very close to him. He was pawing at his chest and great red welts were coming up on his purplish neck. The fact that he didn't make much noise was the most shocking. I guess he was trying to mouth my name as he looked at me through bulging shiny eyes, but all that came out was a sort of crackling noise.

His left hand swiped out at me, then brushed across the off-white carpet. I don't know why I didn't run or even call for help. He was fading, I knew that much, but his arm kept flailing back and forth across the carpet, like he was making a quarter of a snow angel, except there was no snow, only off-white shag, covered by shells, walnut shells. I looked around and saw the overturned wooden bowl, given him by an admirer, along with his monogrammed cracker (another fan's gift) scattered on the floor amid the shards of walnut shell. I was shocked when he began making noises again, not so loud now, more of a gurgling—almost my name, but not quite. I pressed my hand hard against my mouth, not out of fear, horror, or panic. I was laughing. Laughing not because he was choking to death, but that he was choking to death on walnuts. I remember, in the rush of emergency personnel and my mother's howling that followed, feeling slightly horrified with myself. As horrified as I had felt when he had come to my school for a lecture and singled me out as his son. The son of Wally Walnut.

Epilogue

Many years have passed since then. As I said, I finished University, moved out of town, got a job, married, had a kid—a son of my own. It's taken me a while to come to terms with the man who was my father. Certainly, he meant well, provided for the family, and in this world, the most interesting people are often misunderstood, even by their own children. I carry quite a suitcase of guilt around with me, thinking back about the entirety of my father and his work, his *real* work. Maybe I wasn't the best son either. Sometimes I wake up in the middle of the night, after a bad dream, a memory—my dad, lying on the floor sweeping uselessly through walnut shells, and gasping for air. My therapist suggested I should honour his memory, even if I didn't always enjoy him while he was alive. So, I've decided to carry on a tradition, a family tradition. I named my son after my father. It was the best I could do. What did you think? Really, you must be nuts to get an idea like that in your head. Are you serious? Become Wally Walnut the second? What do you think this is, a comic book? Get real…. you've seen too many movies…

Men Cubed

A man in an undershirt, at a window, in an apartment, over a bar. Affordable rent for an affable man. Not even a proper stove, nor a fridge, and barely a toilet. Very much the archetypical bachelor pad. For food, the man ate sardines, fresh from the tin, and peanuts and meat sticks from the bar below. Needless to say, he was a very salty fellow indeed. He had given up a lot just to live in that locale. No, he wasn't a frustrated writer, nor a sweaty musician, just a man who spent a lot of time drinking apple juice and staring out the window. Opposite the bar, encircled by a barbed wire fence, squatted a large prison, a women's correctional institution to be precise. Did he long for someone? Yes, but not a mother, sister, daughter, but for a prospective family member. A wife. Not his per se, but someone who he hoped would be his life partner, who hopefully wouldn't be in for life. From his vantage point, the man watched the prison gates, captivated.

Regulars at the bar below thought the man a quiet harmless oddity, a greasy blur on the subconscious, rarely even discussed, except by way of explanation to a newcomer. Ritually, as the news came on a noon, barstools creaked and turned to allow sodden red eyes an accustomed sight. The man, now with a golf shirt and combed hair, would stand at attention before the gates of the prison, convenience store chocolates in one hand sad clutch of wilting flowers in the other. Eyes fixed with beleaguered hope on the entrance to the jail. Every day at this time, a group of different, but similarly relieved women were escorted to the gate by two uniformed matrons. With a slight and salty smile on his face, the man nodded a wordless hello to each of them as they went on their way to husbands, boyfriends, family, or to a male void, which some of them preferred. The last, and smallest percentage were the single ones, in search of the right one. The man wanted some day to encounter one of these women, in a love at first sight scenario, and take her away to a happy home.

The man had become somewhat of a celebrity for all the wrong reasons at the bar. He drew chortles from the patrons as he drew draught lager through his red, chapped lips. It was here he came daily, after the prison gates had closed, and the guards had retreated, shaking their heads at the strange, but inoffensive man. Flowers in the garbage can, chocolates on the bar for any takers, he sat there, drinking slowly and steadily—just enough to fall asleep to. He barely reacted to the occasional tired jeer aimed his way, the jokes falling off him like dust balls. Certainly, there were better places to meet women, or failing that, prostitutes, but to wait for love in front of a women's prison seemed the nadir of desperation. The regulars in the bar shook their heads and laughed, but the man ignored them, confident in the knowledge that he was betting on the slow and steady approach, combined with the law of averages. Sooner or later there would come the one who could see him for what he truly was, an inherently good, mild, balding middle-aged mad who consumed too much sodium. And her. She would be fresh from incarceration, humbled, perhaps angry at the world, and he would take her away from the pain and suffering to a new life.

He loved to watch time pass, particularly digital time. Expectant, hesitant, but always reassuringly consistent, the red blotches of LED crystal would magically transform from one thing to another, transfiguring themselves in a combined space into the next number. The small alarm clock by his bed served as both sport and entertainment. His favourite time was 12:34, am or pm was inconsequential. 1, 2, 3, 4, all in a row, for one minute exactly, but no seconds please, too messy. He chided himself for missing either of the two daily performances, and especially both. He was usually at work at noon, and half asleep when the new day came. Still, with a childlike urgency, he pressed on his timely horse, and silently cheered as his runner moved into the winning spot. In truth, his little world revolved around this mildly obsessive trait, enamored as he was by a simple chemical and electric process invented years ago—not that he was a technologically minded individual. His fetish remained stable and bland, as long as there was an adequate supply of power. A minute would always be a minute, an imposed yardstick on eternity, but to this man, it was a mad race to the finish line. Only to begin again. A never-ending contest with apparently no winner. The man did not think of his past time as a wasted stop on the bus route of life, but as a comfort and a true joy. Clocks were scattered all over his one chaired apartment, he had no real friends to speak of, no other interests other than his strange hobby and maintaining basic human needs, paying bills, going to work, and living through time.

In a little office, a man sat in the waiting room at one of the three chairs designed for sitting uncomfortably. The room smelt of stale despair and anxiety, neither of which showed on the man's face. Only a slight and satisfied smile rested there, childlike, floating over his smooth, shiny skin. He read no magazines, shuffled no papers, and twiddled no thumbs. When called upon to enter a room marked "AUDITS" the man did so willingly, with a spring in his step as he rose sprightly. Nestling himself in a more comfortable chair, albeit worn around the arm rests, he faced his interrogator with a fearless, wide smile. "Sir" began the intense man behind the desk, "May I be quite frank with you?". "Sure, you can!" replied the man, with a faint musical lilt in his voice. Sighing, the official continued "According to our records, you have never filed for income tax, and, in turn, now owe a sum totaling over fifteen thousand dollars. The other man said nothing, but jerked one eyebrow upwards and shrugged his shoulders quickly, hands upraised. The auditor behind the desk furrowed his brow and, after a pause, leaned across the desk, his voice lowered "So you have nothing to say about this?" A polite and simple "Nope!" was the reply. The official coughed dryly into his hand. "Therefore, am I to assume that you will NOT be paying the full, or even a partial amount of the monies due?", eyebrow twitching on 'not'. "I dunno…" came the unsophisticated reply. With an extra-large inhale, the auditor continued, "And what, exactly, is the reasoning behind this, if I may ask, *sir*?". The man across the desk from him clapped his hands excitedly, and began to explain himself in an animated manner, bordering on the juvenile.

"Well!", the man started, slapping his left knee "When I was about six years old, I climbed up the wrong diving board, you now, the highest one at the swimming pool." He mimicked surprise mixed with fear "And I couldn't go down, because there were people behind me, so I walked to the end of the board and looked down" he jerked his head towards the floor in imitation. "Everyone was yelling at me, telling me to jump, but I was… so… scared!" lifting his head now, "So, I held my breath… and…" he was staring now, somewhat wild-eyed at his accuser, and, lifting his arms, shouted "I jumped! I did it! I jumped!" This climactic, high-pitched finale sent the man up from his seat, and back down again, with a triumphant "Sploosh!". The entire scene seemed to be carefully rehearsed, or at least performed by the man many, many times.

Justifiably nonplussed, the official, who would of course repeat this story many times at social gatherings, now tapped the side of his thin nose. Searching for something to say, he reverted to his previous question "So, if I understand correctly, you're not going to pay the amount then? The other man, still breathless, replied by smiling and shaking his head, and, as if in answer to the stunned auditors next question, the strange man continued "Well, I figure this", he began, raising one index finger in the air. "If I did something as great as that, then I don't have to do anything else for a little while at least!" As far as explanations went, this one was extremely hollow, a thin patina between reality and evasion. This docile refusal followed a trail of lawsuits, alimony, palimony, car wrecks, abandoned businesses, and now an onerous tax bill. "Well, I'm sure you know the consequences of defaulting on your payments sir?" "Sure do!".

At this, the official cleared his throat "All I can say to you sir, that in my professional opinion I hope you reconsider, otherwise you will be faced with extra penalties in addition to the amount owing, and perhaps even jail time." he said, trying to put on a caring face. The odd, beaming man smiled, and leaned forward, conspiringly, and bid the tax accountant do the same. They were level now, across the great wooden desk, chin to perspiring chin. "Don't worry!" the man whispered, coming even closer now, "I'm going sky diving this weekend!"

Hamilton Poem

A golden phoenix of azure brilliance
rises in the East to meet my walking
feet.
The Echoes of workingmen's footsteps remind
me that this is a city
of production, of productivity.

From the heights of Hamilton Mountain, not unlike
Olympus to the watery blessed shores of the beautiful,
bountiful bay.
The hustle and bustle of the city centre
a veritable microcosm, where all manner of merchants
dwell, to sell their wares to travelers from near and far.

A single sparrow speaks to me of
the beauty of Bayfront. The tenacity of Bold Street.
The royalty of
James, and the
glory of Gage.
Not forgetting, of course, the straightforwardness of Hunter

Oh dear, I seem to be in the wrong poem. Pardon me!
Whimsy and wade in as you may, but I see Hamilton in a different way.

I see two middle-aged men hitting each other with sticks in the old GO station parking lot, one of them is wearing an undershirt that reads, you guessed it "Welcome to Hamilton."

I hear people coming home from the bars—old men's' bars, young men's' bars, cheap bars, chic bars, mean bars, and nice bars, where everybody knows your name.

I smell whatever THAT is, from one of a hundred sources.

I feel at home.

Living in an apartment directly over top of a payphone at Main and Wentworth—no explanations necessary. Discount stores discounting other discount stores' discountability. How many times can one put the word 'Bargain' on a sign?

Phrases like: "He was supposed to cut me a check!", "Aw, he's good people.", and "No he's not, he's a fucking goof!"

The last one a crossed Rubicon, as if one man had defecated on the other's best China.

Being recognized (mistakenly) from prison on more than one occasion.

Being recognized and never having met the person in question, in jail or otherwise. "Hey, where's my twenty bucks!"

Having more than once not known how I got home.

Small wonders in dusty second-hand bookshops, unhindered by alphabetical constraints. Patronizing mom n' pop diners, where one can haggle over the price of a breakfast.

Getting the feeling that minding my own business is a good idea. Hearing some great sounds in some awful clubs.

Being asked by others why I live here, and just smiling by way of an answer. I pretend there's some sort of secret

Which will never pass my lips, a dirty kind of secret.

A Hamilton kind of secret, that not even the high cab drivers will let you know, as they drop the beer off at 4 am in the morning.

Take 'er easy, buddy.

**IT'S CONTEST TIME!!!
FINISH THE STORY
IN 500 WORDS OR LESS
EMAIL SUBMISSIONS TO:
jeffscribbler@gmail.com**

**WINNER WILL BE ANNOUNCED AND PRINTED
IN *A NASTY PIECE OF WORK* VOL 2**

Judy Robinson was shopping in the dollar store for a pregnancy test when everything she had ever known or understood came crashing down. Just like that.

Printed in the USA
CPSIA information can be obtained
at www.ICGtesting.com
LVHW040512280324
775676LV00037B/244

9 781039 198265